Pathfinder 38

CW00840849

Pairwork:
interaction in the modern languages classroom

The Pathfinder *Series*

Active learning — listening and reading

Developing skills for independent reading (PF22)
Iain Mitchell & Ann Swarbrick   ISBN 1 874016 34 8

Creative use of texts (PF21)
Bernard Kavanagh & Lynne Upton   ISBN 1 874016 28 3

Listening in a foreign language (PF26)
A skill we take for granted?
Karen Turner   ISBN 1 874016 44 5

Stimulating grammatical awareness (PF33)
A fresh look at language acquisition
Heather Rendall   ISBN 1 902031 08 3

More reading for pleasure in a foreign language (PF36)
Ann Swarbrick   ISBN 1 902031 13 X

Supporting learners and learning

Teaching learners how to learn
Strategy training in the ML classroom (PF31)
Vee Harris   ISBN 1 874016 83 6

Making effective use of the dictionary (PF28)
Gwen Berwick & Phil Horsfall   ISBN 1 874016 60 7

Nightshift (PF20)
Ideas and strategies for homework
David Buckland & Mike Short   ISBN 1 874016 19 4

Grammar matters (PF17)
Susan Halliwell   ISBN 1 874016 12 7

On course for GCSE coursework (PF35)
Julie Adams   ISBN 1 902031 26 1

Pairwork (PF38)
Interaction in the modern languages classroom
Wendy Phipps   ISBN 1 902031 28 8

Planning and organising teaching

Assessment and planning in the MFL department (PF29)
Harmer Parr   ISBN 1 874016 71 2

Getting the best results at GCSE (PF39)
Mike Buckby & Kate Corney   ISBN 1 902031 27 X

Foreign Language Assistants (PF32)
A guide to good practice
*David Rowles, Marian Carty
& Anneli McLachlan*   ISBN 1 874016 95 X

Improve your image (PF15)
The effective use of the OHP
Daniel Tierney & Fay Humphreys   ISBN 1 874016 04 6

Teaching/learning in the target language

On target (PF5)
Teaching in the target language
Susan Halliwell & Barry Jones   ISBN 0 948003 54 5

Keeping on target (PF23)
Bernardette Holmes   ISBN 1 874016 35 5

Words (PF34)
Teaching and learning vocabulary
David Snow   ISBN 1 902031 14 8

Motivating all learners

Yes — but will they behave? (PF4)
Managing the interactive classroom
Susan Halliwell   ISBN 0 948003 44 8

Not bothered? (PF16)
Motivating reluctant language learners in Key Stage 4
Jenifer Alison   ISBN 1 874016 06 2

Differentiation and individual learners (PF37)
A guide for classroom practice
Anne Convery & Do Coyle   ISBN 1 902031 10 5

Cultural awareness

Crossing frontiers (PF30)
The school study visit abroad
David Snow & Michael Byram   ISBN 1 874016 84 4

Exploring otherness (PF24)
An approach to cultural awareness
Barry Jones   ISBN 1 874016 42 9

Broadening the learning experience

New contexts for modern language learning (PF27)
Cross-curricular approaches
Kim Brown & Margot Brown   ISBN 1 874016 50 X

With a song in my scheme of work (PF25)
Steven Fawkes   ISBN 1 874016 45 3

Drama in the languages classroom (PF19)
Judith Hamilton & Anne McLeod   ISBN 1 874016 07

Being Creative (PF10)
Barry Jones   ISBN 0 948003 99 5

All Pathfinders are available through good book suppliers or direct from **Grantham Book Services**, Isaac Newton Way, Alma Park Industrial Estate, Grantham, Lincs NG31 9SD.
Fax orders to: 01476 541 061. Credit card orders: 01476 541 080

Pathfinder 38

A CILT series for language teachers

Pairwork

Interaction in the modern languages classroom

Wendy Phipps

Centre for Information
on Language Teaching and Research

The views expressed in this publication are the author's and do not necessarily represent those of CILT.

First published 1999
Copyright © 1999 Centre for Information on Language Teaching and Research
ISBN 1 902031 28 8

A catalogue record for this book is available from the British Library
Printed in Great Britain by Copyprint UK Ltd

Illustrations by Genna Hollins

Published by the Centre for Information on Language Teaching and Research,
20 Bedfordbury, Covent Garden, London WC2N 4LB

CILT Publications are available from: Grantham Book Services, Isaac Newton Way, Alma Park Industrial Estate, Grantham, Lincs NG31 8SD. Tel: 01476 541 080. Fax: 01476 541 061. Book trade representation (UK and Ireland): Broadcast Book Services, 24 De Montfort Road, London SW16 1LZ. Tel: 0181 677 5129.

All rights reserved. No part of this publication may be reproduced, stored in a retrieval system, or transmitted in any form or by any means, electronic, mechanical, photographic, recording, or otherwise, without the prior permission of the Copyright owner.

Contents

Introduction: Why pairwork?

When was the last time you had a conversation with someone and there were thirty others (or more) listening in? We as teachers expect our pupils to do exactly this when asking them to speak out in front of the class. Some of our pupils will of course thoroughly enjoy this experience, but others will grimly stare at the desk in fervent hope of not being asked to answer the next question.

Working with a partner is much less intimidating than being singled out to answer in front of the class, and it brings a realistic element into the classroom by simulating the natural conversational setting.

This Pathfinder sets out to examine the nature of pairwork and to give teachers a comprehensive and practical overview of what can be achieved through the use of pairwork in the modern languages classroom.

Pairwork can be defined as . . .

> . . . a convenient short term for any form of pupi–pupil interaction without the intervention of the teacher.[1]

This definition provides a useful starting point for exploring the many and varied possibilities of creating situations which enable pupils to work with one another independently of the teacher.

HOW DOES IT BENEFIT OUR PUPILS?

Pairwork is a very efficient way of learning in respect of how we learn.

As learners it is thought that we take in:

10% of what we read
20% of what we hear
30% of what we see
50% of what we see and hear
70% of what we ourselves say and
90% of what we ourselves do [2]

Thus by increasing opportunities for pupils to speak and work on their own and to take a more active part in the learning process, we will increase the likelihood of their retaining the language they are learning.

> Pairwork gives pupils a chance to improvise real life situations. Roleplay is virtually the only way we can give our learners the opportunity to practise improvising a range of real life spoken language in the classroom, and it is an extremely effective technique if the students are confident and co-operative . . . [3]

> Pairwork maximises the time available for pupils to communicate: the opportunity for interaction between the teacher and any one pupil is strictly limited, whereas pupil–pupil interaction gives every pupil the chance to communicate actively.[1]

Pairwork gives pupils independence, it reinforces language and it takes the onus off the teacher.

> Pairwork is essential for language teaching . . . It is important that the onus is off the teacher at times, and on the children. Secondly, it is important that the children . . . have the responsibility for their own learning and . . . independence, which I feel they benefit from. Thirdly, it reinforces so well anything that you have done with the class initially.[4]

Working with other pupils is perceived as a key way of how pupils should learn according to the National Curriculum documentation.

Under the heading *Communicating in the target language* the document states:

Pupils should be given opportunities to:

- *communicate with each other in pairs and groups, and with their teacher;*
- *develop their understanding and skills through a range of language activities, e.g.* **games, roleplay, surveys and other investigations** *(their emphasis);*
- *take part in imaginative and creative activities, e.g. improvised drama;*
- *discuss their own ideas, interests and experiences and compare them with those of others; and*
- *use a range of resources for communicating, e.g. telephone, electronic mail, fax, letters.*

Under the second heading *Language skills* the document states that pupils should be taught to:

- *ask and answer questions and give instructions;*
- *ask for and give information and explanations;*
- *initiate and develop conversations;*
- *express agreement, disagreement, personal feelings and opinions; and*
- *describe and discuss present, past and future events.[5]*

Buckby et al (1992) in *Learning strategies* lay out very clearly eight stages in the learning process. These are:

Stage 1 – setting objectives
Stage 2 – introducing language
Stage 3 – imitating
Stage 4 – repeating
Stage 5 – understanding patterns in language
Stage 6 – manipulating
Stage 7 – producing and creating language
Stage 8 – assessment and evaluation[4]

The stages of imitation, repetition, manipulating and creativity (Stages 3, 4, 5 & 7) are of particular interest in respect of pairwork.

IMITATION
Here the learner says the words aloud, immediately after a spoken model, or reads aloud a written or printed model.[4]

REPETITION
Pupils imitate new language by copying an immediate model (immediate being considered as within the three to ten seconds of the short-term memory). Gradually, as their confidence and competence grow, the time gap can be increased so that there is no immediate model. We can then say that the pupils have reached the learning step of repetition. Initially the gap may only be a few seconds, but it will gradually increase to minutes, hours, days, weeks and months.[4]

MANIPULATION
In this stage, instead of just learning a phrase, pupils adapt that phrase and put it into another situation. Therefore we have them moving away from rote learning to producing something more creative which is obviously more interesting. I think the pupils get a lot more out of being able to say something that they want to say.[4]

> **CREATIVITY**
>
> Creative use of language can be a modest exclamation or an ambitious project.
>
> A further element in the definition of creativity . . . is concerned with activities which encourage learners to use their imagination and to involve themselves as thinking, feeling, imagining human beings — an aspect which is the essence of real life communication.[4]

Pairwork can be used at every stage of the language learning process. It is applicable from the early stages of **imitation** and **repetition** right through to the stage when pupils are **creating** their own language. We will see that we can usefully get our pupils interacting with one another throughout the whole learning process, thereby involving them, and so hopefully holding their interest in all that is done in the languages classroom.

In summary then:

Pairwork . . .

- reduces the amount of teacher/whole class talk;
- consolidates the learning process;
- promotes involvement;
- promotes communication;
- promotes social interaction;
- is learner-centred;
- gives pupils the opportunity to work autonomously — thus pupils can work at their own pace and in the privacy of their pair;
- takes the onus off the teacher and frees him/her to address individuals' needs more precisely and intensely.

Pairwork also provides:

- the perfect opportunity to introduce differentiation;
- variety in the classroom activities;
- a different way of working;
- legitimate opportunities for pupils to get up and walk about the room, once again bringing variety into the classroom.

In the following chapters we will look at the various stages of learning and see how different types of pairwork can be introduced at each and every stage.

CiLT

1.   Getting ready for pairwork

Before we do any pairwork activity, we must ensure that our pupils are well prepared for the concept of pairwork, and that they are ready for this exciting and highly efficient way of learning/consolidating language.

This chapter will cover five very important aspects of preparation.

1. Preparing pupils for pairwork from a motivational point of view.
2. Setting out the classroom to accommodate pairwork.
3. Looking at the different organisational ways we can use to facilitate effective pairwork.
4. Working out who should work with whom.
5. Looking at how to achieve the transition from whole class to pairwork.

PREPARING PUPILS FOR PAIRWORK

Initially we must examine our reasons for asking pupils to work in pairs in the first place. From the teacher's point of view the reason for getting pupils to interact will inevitably be seen in linguistic terms, but for the pupils, what is the reason for the activity?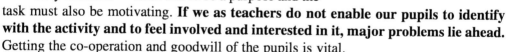

Pupils must have a reason for interacting. The task given to the pupils must be meaningful. This point is absolutely essential — there has to be a purpose and the task must also be motivating. **If we as teachers do not enable our pupils to identify with the activity and to feel involved and interested in it, major problems lie ahead.** Getting the co-operation and goodwill of the pupils is vital.

How do we achieve that?

- **Get pupils involved**

Where appropriate involve them in deciding upon some of the content of the work to be covered, e.g.:

At the beginning of a unit of work on leisure, you can say: '*We'll be looking at what people do in their leisure time over the next three weeks – what sort of activities will you want to talk about?*' You can then ask the pupils which activities they want to include in the work they will be doing. This can be done by brainstorming the class for their suggestions (in target language and/or English depending on the level/ability of the pupils). Alternatively, you can ask pupils to write down on a piece of paper activities which they personally will want to talk about. Take in all of the suggestions and make sure to include all the activities mentioned by the class.

You can then go on to say that they will want to find out what other people do in their spare time and ask for suggestions about how the class can best get this information. Suggestions such as interviewing your partner, doing a class survey, interviewing friends and family will all most probably come up in this type of discussion.

The fact that the pupils themselves have come up with the ideas and the fact that the teacher will then go on to incorporate some of these suggestions into the unit of work means that the pupils feel from the start that it is their work and something they want to do.

- **Give pupils a choice of activity where possible**

For pupils to be fully involved, they need to feel that they have some say in what they do. There will be times, naturally, when the teacher will want everyone to be doing the same activity in the same way at the same time, but where possible give pupils a choice in what they do.

How does this work in practice?

Speaking activities in pairs: provide a selection of activities which can be graded in difficulty or provide different types of activity which are all at the same level of difficulty. These activities could be on cards which are colour coded, e.g. everyone starts with the blue cards (a basic roleplay activity) but then can choose from the green, yellow or red cards.

Green — the same roleplay, but pupils are asked to act out the dialogue using different emotions, e.g. anger, frustration etc.

Yellow — pupils are asked to change words in the dialogue, selecting items from a pool of words. They may also change other parts of the dialogue (times, dates, prices and location, change names of those participating in dialogue).

C*i*LT

Red — pupils are asked to illustrate the dialogue in pictures and symbols, thus creating their own cue card in symbol form.

Introducing such differentiated activities as mentioned above contributes greatly to securing the pupils' involvement. Providing tasks graded in difficulty enables pupils to work at their own pace and level of ability. Providing different types of activity at the same level of difficulty gives pupils a certain freedom in that they have a choice in what they do. Both these elements – providing tasks at an appropriate level and, where possible, providing choice – are conducive to pupil satisfaction.

- **Encourage pupils to 'play the game'**

If we are successful in getting the co-operation of the pupils, we will, hopefully, have achieved the goal of getting pupils to play the game and to accept that:

- they do have to 'play act';
- the situation is artificial;
- they won't look at their partner's information; and
- they won't 'cheat'.

Handled correctly, playing the game will be seen as a very positive aspect of the work.

From the teacher's point of view — pupils are learning to interact with one another; to co-operate with one another; and the onus is, however briefly, off the teacher.

From the pupil's point of view — they are creating something of their own; they are bringing drama into the classroom; and they have a legitimate excuse to walk around and/or talk to their partner during lesson time!

SETTING OUT THE CLASSROOM

Organising a wide range of successful pairwork activities in your classroom requires you to consider a variety of options which will allow your pupils access to one another and to as much space as possible. Here are a few possibilities to consider:

(i) the single horseshoe

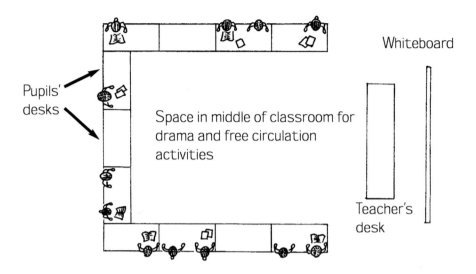

Whiteboard

Pupils' desks

Space in middle of classroom for drama and free circulation activities

Teacher's desk

(ii) the double horseshoe

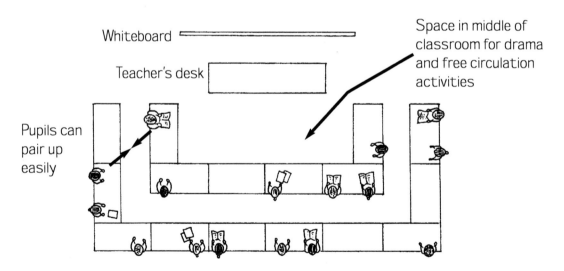

Whiteboard

Teacher's desk

Space in middle of classroom for drama and free circulation activities

Pupils can pair up easily

CiLT

(iii) groups of tables seating four to six pupils

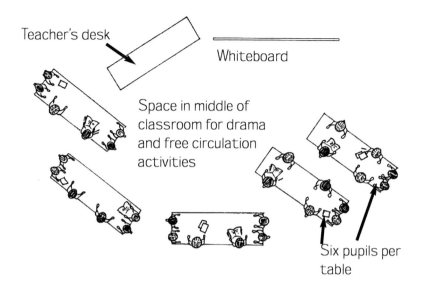

Teacher's desk

Whiteboard

Space in middle of classroom for drama and free circulation activities

Six pupils per table

- **Some other considerations**

You must decide where you will store the resources to which pupils will need access when they do pairwork activities.

You may wish to establish a quiet area in your classroom where pupils can record dialogues or work on the computer, read or listen with headsets.

If you wish to organise a carousel of activities, you must consider how this will fit in with the above arrangements.

ORGANISATION

Working with a partner does not necessarily mean working with the same person for the duration of a pairwork activity. Here are a few other possibilities to consider when setting up your pairwork situations:

- **Free circulation**

This method allows pupils to walk around the classroom interacting with a variety of pupils — finding out, collecting or exchanging information, greeting one another or expressing opinions. It provides an excellent and legitimate opportunity for pupils to get out of their seats and thus get some variety into what can otherwise be a rather rigid 'sitting session'.

From the linguistic viewpoint, free circulation enables pupils to practise the same language over and over again, but because it is always with a different person and the pupils are exchanging or collecting information, the activity is meaningful for the pupil and therefore the repetition is readily accepted as part and parcel of the activity.

Activities:
— pupils greeting one another;
— doing a survey;
— finding the person in the room who has been given the same piece of information as you, etc.

Moving around in inner and outer circles

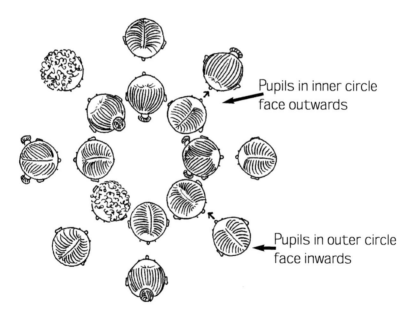

Pupils in inner circle face outwards

Pupils in outer circle face inwards

This arrangement allows you to exercise a little more control over the wanderings of your pupils than the free circulation model permits. However, placing pupils into an inner and an outer circle still allows for a good deal of interaction.

CiLT

Those in the inner circle and those in the outer circle move in an anti-clockwise or clockwise direction according to your instructions. This gives you a high degree of control, yet still allows for a constant change of partners as and when you wish.

Activities:
All the pupils in the inner and outer circles are holding a flashcard, each one with a different type of weather symbol. The pupils move according to the instructions of the teacher.

When they are told to stop, they must ask the person opposite a question, e.g. *Wie ist das Wetter heute*? (What is the weather like today?) Their partner answers the questions and then asks theirs.

A variety of quick-fire activities can take place using this simple rotation method — pupils can greet one another, find out what number each pupil has written down, ask each other their names, how they are feeling today etc.

Pupils face one another seated in two straight rows

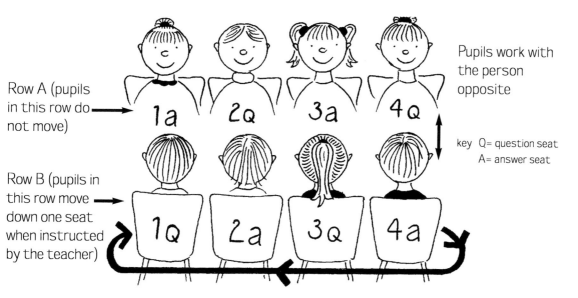

Row A (pupils in this row do not move)

1a 2q 3a 4q

Row B (pupils in this row move down one seat when instructed by the teacher)

1q 2a 3q 4a

Pupils work with the person opposite

key Q= question seat
A= answer seat

This is a variation of the previous exercise. Once again this activity is strictly controlled by the teacher. No-one moves to another seat until the teacher tells them to do so.

This type of seating arrangement is ideal for pairwork activities which involve a series of questions.

Each seat is designated as either a **question seat** or an **answer seat**. As pupils move up and down the rows (only at your command), they have the opportunity to experience the following:

— constant change of partners;
— constant change of topic/set of questions and answers;
— constant change between asking and answering questions (for pupils in Row B only as pupils in Row A do not move).

This activity also allows pupils to work at their own pace. There may be as many as 20 questions on each topic, but pupils only complete what they have time to do with each partner before they are moved on by you.

Examples of questions and answers, which could be used:

Seat 1 = questions and answers on personal information
Seat 2 = leisure activities
Seat 3 = future plans
Seat 4 = last year's holidays

- **Half the class seated**

This allows more freedom for the pupils (well, for those who are not seated.) Those pupils who are standing visit the seated pupils to carry out whatever activity is required.

This arrangement of half the class seated and half the class free to walk round makes a very good basis for a variety of simulation exercises/roleplay work.

Activities:
The *seated half* of the class can be divided into pairs and sit at different points round the classroom. Each pair can represent shopkeepers in different types of shops. They have information or objects or flashcards indicating what is for sale. They also have a list of prices. The job of the seated pupils is to sell their items.

CiLT

The rest of the class represents the customers. They go round (either in pairs or singly depending on the size of the group) with a shopping list. Their task is to visit the various shops and to purchase the items on the shopping list. They must find out and note down the price of each item on their list.

Other possible scenarios:
travel agents — finding out about hotels and flights to different countries;
estate agents — finding out about different types of houses (detached, semi-detached, terrace, bungalows, flats) in different parts of the country;
different types of restaurants — opening hours, menu prices, contents of menus, catering for children, options for vegetarians etc.
cinemas — films and times of opening, prices, reductions for children, OAPs, special offers;
leisure centres— facilities available, opening times.

In each case the *seated half* of the class has the information which the rest of the class needs.

• **The chain**

This is perhaps not strictly what we immediately think of as pairwork, but as it involves interaction with other pupils, it complies, albeit loosely, with the definition stated at the outset.

The chain refers to any activity that involves pupils passing on and/or receiving information or items to or from other pupils.

Activities:
Chinese whispers — where one word or phrase is whispered from one pupil to the next round the class;

Pass the object — where pupils pass items or flashcards to one another naming these items as they hand them over;

Question and answer — e.g. person A to person B ¿*Cómo te llamas*? (What is your name?) person B, *me llamo Anne* (My name is Anne) and then Anne turns to person C ¿*Cómo te llamas*? . . . and so it continues round the class;

Pupil reaction — pupils react to what a previous pupil has just said — word association games, memory games, etc.

The language content of 'chain' work can range from the simple to the very difficult. From the organisational viewpoint the chain is a very controlled type of exercise, as the pupils are not required to move out of their seats.

Working out who works with whom

This is a most important aspect in order to avoid chaos, anarchy and general ill feeling in the classroom! How do we organise who will work with whom in such a way that the class remains 'with' you, the teacher, and does not undermine your best laid plans and efforts by uncooperative and surly behaviour? We must firstly consider the following:

- **Pupils need to feel comfortable with their partners**
Yet at the same time they must become aware from day one that the whole activity of pairwork requires working with a variety of people. We must work hard in the early days to make this mixing with other members of the class a natural and integral part of the language class and one that pupils accept and hopefully enjoy.

- **Flexibility in forming pairs is essential**
As stated above, pupils must get used to working with different people. Sometimes it will be appropriate for pupils to work with a friend, but at other times you may wish to form pairs where a more able pupil can support a weaker pupil. On other occasions it may be most appropriate for pupils of the same ability to work together.

If we can make the above a reality in our classroom, then we have the following choices open to us as teachers to suit the very varied aspects of the work we wish to do.

SUGGESTIONS FOR SELECTING PARTNERS:

You pre-select pupils to work together but make it appear that the choice is random.
This pre-selection can be achieved by allotting pupils a number or a colour or the name of an item at the beginning of the lesson. Then, when it is time to work in pairs, red and yellow work together or numbers 22 and 9 or the banana and the pear. This allows you to select carefully who should work with whom and yet it appears a totally random selection as far as the pupils are concerned, and therefore is more acceptable to them.

You select at random

Pupils can be asked to form pairs by using the following criteria:

— drawing numbers out of a hat;
— getting pupils to line up according to their date and month of birth and you then pair them off accordingly;
— alphabetically by first name or surname.

Pupils will more readily accept being put into a pair — even if they are not with a friend — if they feel that the selection was just the luck of the draw.

Pupils work with their neighbour

Pupils select their own partners

You create a carousel of partners

Here, half the class remains seated and the other half of the class progresses from one partner to the next after an allotted period of time. This system can only work if the classroom allows for pupils to circulate easily around the room, e.g. a horseshoe shape arrangement.

 ## THE TRANSITION FROM WHOLE-CLASS TO PAIRWORK

A fundamental and vitally important aspect of preparation is how we achieve a smooth transition from 30 individual pupils dependent on their teacher to 15 totally independent pairs which allows the teacher the freedom to circulate and monitor the work being done.

Factors that can contribute to a roleplay's success are:
— making sure that the language demanded is well within the learners' capacity;
— your own enthusiasm;
— careful and clear presentation and instructions; a preliminary demonstration or rehearsal by you together with a student volunteer.[1]

Pupils need to have a clear idea of what is expected of them and their partners and what the rules of the games are (see 'A checklist for successful pairwork' on p18).

What does this mean in practice?

We can take for example a basic exchange of information, involving two people, that would occur at a restaurant to show how this independence can gradually be achieved.

Au restaurant conversation

Garçon: Qu'est-ce que vous prenez pour commencer?
Client: Je prends le jambon.
Garçon: Et comme plat principal?
Client: Le poulet, s'il vous plaît.
Garçon: Et comme légumes?
Client: Les frites et les haricots verts.
Garçon: Et comme boisson?
Client: Une carafe de vin rouge, s'il vous plaît.
Garçon: Oui, bien sûr, Monsieur.

To enable the class to work well in pairs on this type of exchange of information, the following preparation must be done with the whole classs:

- The pupils need to be made familiar with each structure and all the vocabulary. This will be achieved gradually by using a wide variety of imitation and repetition techniques with the whole class, with groups in the class and with individual pupils using picture flashcards or some other type of visual prompt to represent the various foods and key phrases which need to be learnt.

- Only when the class is confident with all the individual structures and items of vocabulary can the teacher begin to bring all the elements together to produce a complete exchange of information/conversation.

There is a sequence of steps which needs to be followed to enable pupils to move from this total dependence on the teacher to the independence which is needed before a speaking pairwork activity of this kind can meaningfully and successfully take place.

Steps to independence for pairwork speaking activity:

Example — a restaurant roleplay (see above conversation):

Step 1   Initially you (the teacher) may take on the role of the waiter inviting the whole class or groups within the class to answer your questions. Use a visual stimulus for each question to guide pupils to the answer they should give.

Step 2   Still in your role as waiter, you can then proceed to ask individual pupils to answer your questions. Here again you can provide them with a visual prompt.

Step 3   You now reverse roles and ask the whole class to play the part of the waiter while you play the part of the customer. Once again, have a variety of visual stimuli to guide pupils to the appropriate responses or questions.

Step 4   You now select individual pupils to give the questions and responses of the waiter, while you continue to play the part of the customer.

Step 5   At this point you begin to let go the reins. Half the class is invited to play the part of the waiter and the other half of the class to play the part of the customer. You provide the visual stimuli to guide the conversation and are there to help when required.

Step 6   Individual pupils are now asked to play the parts of the waiter and the customer — from the safety of their seats if they wish. The rest of the class listens. One pupil can take on the whole role of the waiter/customer or can share it with several other pupils. You are there to guide and to provide the prompts as and when required. You can ask several pairs of pupils to do the role play until you are satisfied that the class as a whole is confident with the structures and the vocabulary.

It is only after this series of steps have taken place that pupils are now ready to work on the restaurant conversation in pairs and you can say with confidence: '*Et maintenant avec ton partenaire!*'

A CHECKLIST FOR SUCCESSFUL PAIRWORK

1. Show enthusiasm as a teacher.

2. Choose work or tasks which are at the right level.

3. Provide thorough preparation.
Language used in pairwork needs to have been thoroughly practised beforehand with the whole class as in the example of the 'six steps to independence' described for the restaurant conversation.

4. Give clear teacher instructions.
Pupils must know exactly what is expected of them and what the role of each partner is. If necessary, instructions such as these should be given before a pairwork activity begins, e.g. *'Du bist Partner A, du bist Partner B. Partner A beginnt. Beginnt jetzt!'* ('You are Partner A, you are Partner B (pointing to each pupil to make sure they all know their roles). Partner A begins. Begin now!')

5. Make manageable pairwork rules.
— Pupils should be trained to get into their pairs quickly, quietly and without fuss. They should also be trained to go back quickly to whole class work in the same way.

— Pupils must know exactly what is expected of them in respect of behaviour when working with a partner in relation to:

- use of target language;
- acceptable noise level;
- work to be achieved;
- sanctions if rules are not adhered to.

— If pupils are required to move around the classroom, then it must be made totally clear to them exactly what they should be doing and the behaviour expected of them.

If the teacher wants the attention of the whole class during a pairwork activity, it is essential that the teacher works out a system with the class to achieve this.

2. Pairwork based on speaking

In this chapter we will look at the wide variety of activities which pupils can do in pair-work situations as they progress through the learning stages from imitation to repetition to manipulation to production and creativity. (These stages are based on those learning stages identified by Buckby et al (1992).[1]

The activities have been divided into two categories. Firstly into activities where the main emphasis is on speaking, and secondly into activities which involve a mixture of skills.

All the activities in this chapter will have speaking as their main emphasis.

THE IMITATION STAGE

At this stage of learning pupils are limited in their questions and responses and can only replicate the words or sentences they have heard and repeated many times in the whole class situation. However, in order to make this language 'come alive' and become their own, they must have the opportunity to repeat it in a much more personal and realistic way.

Also, at this stage, pairwork will be very limited in terms of language used and also time spent, but this certainly does not mean that it cannot be a very worthwhile activity.

• **Repeat**
Ask pupils to repeat in pairs what they have just repeated chorally as a whole class activity. This can be individual words or phrases which can be enhanced by a mime to explain the word or phrase, e.g. *mir ist übel* (I am feeling sick), or *tengo hambre* (I'm hungry). In pairs pupils can be asked to repeat the phrase and to make up their own action/mime for the ailment/feeling.

• **Circulate round the class**
Pupils can be given a simple task that will involve using the same language with many different people, e.g. they can:

— move round the room and greet fellow pupils, noting down the name of each pupil greeted;

— assume another identity and then circulate round the room to find out everyone's 'new' name;

— be given a number and then circulate round the room to find out which number everyone else has and who in the room has the same number as themselves.

• **Pass the object**
In this type of activity pupils can be involved in passing an object/picture of an object to one another and naming it as they pass the item to the next person.

• **Toss the ball**
Use a softball and ask pupils to throw it to another pupil anywhere in the class. The pupil catching it must say the required word(s) before tossing it to another pupil. The advantage of using the softball exercise is that it keeps the class 'on their toes' — they do not know when it will be their turn to speak.

• **Whisper the word to the back of the row**
A range of flashcards showing pictures of items or illustrating activities are propped up at the front of the class so that everyone can see them. Alternatively, a collection of real items could be placed at the front of the room, once again in full view of all pupils.

You whisper the name of the item/required phrase to a pupil in the front row. This language is then whispered back until it reaches a pupil in the back row who then comes to the front of the class to identify the card or item they think they have heard.

This stage of learning provides an excellent opportunity for pupils to work together in a variety of ways using drama to create actions for words or phrases. Total physical response plays an important part in the early stages of learning and can thus be incorporated into a wealth of pairwork activities.

It is important to note that many of these activities will take only a matter of seconds to complete in some cases, but because such activities allow the individual pupil the chance to personalise and consolidate on a one-to-one basis language which they have just heard and imitated in a whole class situation, they are indeed worthwhile activities.

CiLT

THE REPETITION STAGE

Once pupils have reached the repetition stage, possibilities for pairwork are vastly enhanced. The pupils now possess a repertoire of words and phrases from which to draw. Different and more challenging activities can now be introduced to give them the opportunity to practise and consolidate this language. Here are some ideas:

- **READ ALOUD**

Read against the clock
Seeing how quickly partners can read something aloud, e.g. the alphabet, a list of numbers, months of the year. Pupils time themselves and then see if they can improve on their time.

Read aloud and identify
Partner A reads aloud a time or a number from a list of times or numbers which both partners have in numerical form written down in front of them. Partner B has to identify the time or number as quickly as possible by pointing to what Partner A has just read, e.g. (1) 18.02, 18.03, 18.12 (2) 2.20, 2.10, 3.20 (3) 569, 596, 568 (4) 215, 250, 315.

Read as correctly as possible
A good pronunciation exercise. In this activity partners take it in turns to read aloud words or phrases as correctly as possible. Words which sound similar to one another, words which sound funny, words which are similar to English or words which pupils have difficulty in pronouncing can all be used.

Which words have I changed?
Partner A reads out a text deliberately changing some words in the text, e.g. '*Ich trage einen grünen Pullover*' (I'm wearing a green pullover) when the text in fact reads '*Ich trage einen roten Pullover*' (I'm wearing a red pullover). Partner B must stop partner A and correct him/her as soon as s/he spots a change. Easier changes could be place names or people's names, for example.

Finish my sentence
Partner A and Partner B have both got a copy of the same text. Partner A starts to read aloud from the text and then suddenly stops in mid-sentence, e.g. *Samedi je suis allé à Rouen. Je suis arrivé à . . .* (On Saturday I went to Rouen. I arrived at . . .). Partner B must complete the sentence. Partner B now takes over reading aloud the text until s/he too stops unexpectedly. And so the activity continues.

This is a good exercise for reading and it keeps both partners on their toes as they never know when they will have to 'jump in' and take over the reading. Extra interest is added to this activity by getting the pupils to record themselves – see which pair's recording sounds flawless and uninterrupted!

- **FOLLOWING INSTRUCTIONS**

Do as I say
In this type of activity one partner gives instructions which the other partner must carry out. This gives a wonderful opportunity for pupils to make up a series of mimes and actions to complement verbal instructions, e.g.:

Partner A gives directions: *Geh geradeaus und dann nimm die erste Straße rechts* (go straight ahead and then take the first street on the right) and Partner B acts these directions out. For parts of the body Partner A calls out: *Touche le nez, la bouche etc.* (Touch your nose, mouth etc) and Partner B responds accordingly.

Draw what I say
Very similar to *Do as I say*, but this time the verbal instructions given by Partner A are carried out by Partner B by means of drawings, e.g.:

Partner A and Partner B both have simple maps of a town. Partner A's map has all the buildings drawn on and each building is numbered. Partner B has just got numbered blank spaces. Partner A calls out a numbered blank space and tells Partner B what the building is. Partner B must now draw the building s/he hears, e.g. *numero uno: un super-mercato, numero due: una banca, numero tre: un ufficio postale* (number one: a supermarket, number two: a bank, number three: a post office)

Draw what I say information gap activity
The above activity can of course be changed into an information gap activity requiring both partners to exchange information and draw in missing buildings into the maps on the opposite page in order for each partner to have a complete map:

Partner A would start by asking *che è numero uno?*
Partner B would reply *numero uno è una banca*
Partner A would then draw in the sign for a bank in box no. 1.
Partner A and Partner B continue to ask questions and give answers until both maps are complete.

Key for maps

P = un ufficio postale

i = un ufficio turistico

= un supermercato

= una iglesia

= un café

£ = una banca

Partner A's map   ## Partner B's map

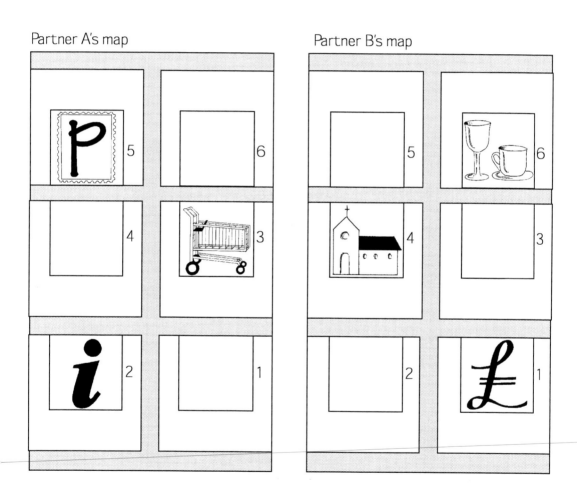

This type of information gap activity can be based on a whole variety of items/tools, e.g. furniture in a room, types of transport, items of food and drink, classroom items, items of clothing, items of lost property, pets, etc.

Draw what I say (but don't look!)

In this activity Partner A is given a blank piece of paper (attached to a board) and a pencil. They hold the board in front of them in such a way that they will not be able to see what they will be drawing. Partner B now gives them instructions for drawing a face, e.g. *el ojo derecho* (the right eye), *la boca* (mouth), *los oídos* (ears), *la garganta* (throat), *la nariz* (nose), *el ojo izquierdo* (the left eye). Partner B continues to give instructions until all the parts of the face have been drawn by Partner A. The end result is usually a wonderfully abstract portrait!

- GUESSING ACTIVITIES

Which word/item have I selected?

A selection of symbols or pictures or objects are on view. Pupil A notes down secretly the item s/he is thinking of from those on show and Pupil B has to try and guess which item his/her partner has selected.

Which phrase/word am I miming?

Pupil A mimes an activity or an emotion from a list of activities/emotions listed on the OHP or in the pupils' text or exercise books. Pupil B guesses what the mime means, e.g.:

Pupil A *mimes an emotion.*
Pupil B: *Estás triste*? (are you sad?)
Pupil A: *No*
Pupil B: *Estás harto*? (are you fed up?)
Pupil A: *Sí* (Yes)

What am I drawing?

Partner A selects an item from a list of items written in the target language. Both partners can see this list. Partner A now starts to draw the item s/he has selected. Partner B has to try and identify the item as quickly as possible by naming it in the target language.

Which word or phrase am I silently 'mouthing'?

Pupil A selects a word or phrase from a list which can be seen by both pupils. S/he

CiLT

silently mouths the word/phrase to Pupil B. Pupil B has to try and identify the word or phrase by the shape of the lip movements Pupil A is making.

- ## MEMORY ACTIVITIES

How many words can you remember?
Pupil A sets out a selection of symbols/pictures/items on the desk for Pupil B to memorise. Pupil B has a minute (or more depending on the number of items/ ability of the pupils) to try and memorise all the items. Pupil A then removes the symbols/pictures. Pupil B must now name the items. As each item is named, Pupil A replaces it on the desk.

Kim's game
This is a variation of the activity above. However, in this game, after all the items have been memorised, the pupil being 'tested' is asked to look away whilst only one item is removed. The pupil now has to try and work out which item is missing.

At the market
This activity involves telling your partner items which you have bought at the market. Pupil A starts by selecting an item of his/her own choosing, e.g. *Ich habe 500 Gramm Käse gekauft* (I bought 500 grammes of cheese). Pupil B now repeats what Pupil A has said and then adds an additional item, e.g. *Ich habe 500 Gramm Käse und 10 Eier gekauft* (I bought 500 grammes of cheese and 10 eggs). And so the activity continues with each partner adding on an additional item.

The items for the game can be selected by pupils purely from memory or can be chosen from a list of symbols/pictures on the OHP. Alternatively, each pair can have their own list of symbols on individual small cards which they place on the desk symbol side up as they select each item. In a different version cards may be placed symbol side down if pupils wish to test their memory of the item as well as the word in the target language.

This activity also works well as a chain game round the class.

Pelmanism games (find the matching pairs)
In pelmanism a set of mini symbol/picture/word or phrase cards are placed face down on the table. There can be as many as 40-50 cards or as few as 10 depending on the ability and/or level of the pupil. The cards are in pairs, i.e. there are pairs of cards which have identical symbols/pictures/words/phrases. The object of the activity is to find as many identical pairs as possible.

At each turn a player is allowed to turn two cards 'face side up' and say out loud what the object is on the card/read aloud what is written on each card. If the two cards match, the player wins the pair and removes them from the table. If the cards are not identical, the player must replace them again face side down. It is now the next player's turn. The object of the game is to win as many pairs of cards as possible. This game provides a stimulating element of competition and ensures that each player pays close attention to each card that is turned up.

Mastermind

Pupils can test one another on vocabulary or phrases by using mini flashcards that have a symbol or picture on one side and the word or phrase in the target language on the other. Partner B is given just 30 seconds or a minute to name all the items of vocabulary shown to him/her in turn in symbol form by Partner A. The object of the activity is to try and name as many flashcards as possible in the given time.

- **INFORMATION GAP ACTIVITIES**

Information gap activities are excellent in that they provide the most important reason for pupils to speak to their partners. Each partner has information which the other is missing and which they need to complete their task. Only by swapping information can they both obtain the full details they need.

Information gap activities can be based on:

- school timetables;
- map of a town (as shown already on page 23);
- diagram of layout of a building, e.g. train station, leisure centre, shopping centre, department store;
- plan of a house showing location of rooms;
- plan of a room showing location of items of furniture;
- menus; bus/train timetables;
- missing items in a picture.

Information gap exercises can also be of the kind outlined on the next page:

CiLT

Who lives where?

Partner A information:

Vorname	Land
John	England
Sven	?
Céline	Frankreich
Thomas	Deutschland
Julie	?
Carlos	Spanien
Richard	?

Partner B information:

Vorname	Land
John	?
Sven	(in der) Schweiz
Céline	?
Thomas	?
Julie	Holland
Carlos	?
Richard	Österreich

In this activity partners take it in turn to find the missing countries on their cards by using the question form *Wo wohnt . . . ?* (Where does [name of person] live?). Partner A will start by asking *Wo wohnt Sven?* Partner B replies *Sven wohnt in der Schweiz* (Sven lives in Switzerland). They continue to ask one another questions until both have completed their cards.

Questionnaires and surveys

Questionnaires and surveys can provide pupils with an opportunity to repeat time and time again the same words and phrases as they ask fellow pupils their likes and dislikes regarding food, films, tv programmes, sports etc.

Survey on brothers and sisters.

In this survey the question is very straightforward:

Tienes hermanos? (do you have any brothers or sisters?)

The pupils make the grid for themselves. They then circulate round the room gathering this information from their fellow pupils and marking it down on the questionnaire as follows:

Nombre	Hermano(s)	Hermana(s)
Andrew	2	—
Julie	1	1
Jayne	1	1

People's views on television programmes.

Once again pupils can construct this grid for themselves very quickly. By circulating round the room they can gather each other's views on a range of programmes. Once the information has been collected, pupils can feed the results back to the teacher as a whole class activity.

Question: *Wie findest du* . . . plus name of television programme? (What do you think of .... ?) e.g. 9 o'clock News, Top of the Pops, Friends etc.

	Friends	Top of the Pops	6 'oclock News	Animal Hospital
1 Ich finde *name of programme* toll I think *name of programme* is great				
2 Ich finde *name of programme* sehr gut I think *name of programme* is very good				
3 Ich finde *name of programme* gut I think *name of programme* is good				
4 Es geht It's OK				
5 Kenn ich nicht I don't watch it				
6 Ich finde *name of programme* nicht gut I don't think *name of programme* is any good				
7 Ich finde *name of programme* gar nicht gut I don't like *name of programme* at all				
8 Ich finde *name of programme* schrecklich I think *name of programme* is dreadful				

A good follow-up exercise would be for pupils to show the results of their survey as a bar graph.

CILT

- **GAMES**

Dice Games

Each number on the dice represents a phrase, a picture, a person, a place etc. A whole host of simple games based on throwing a dice can provide excellent opportunities for pupils to repeat language.

Example:

Partner A asks, 'Where are you?' Partner B throws the dice and, depending on how the dice lands, s/he replies, 'I am in the kitchen, sitting room,' etc.

The level of language used can of course be altered to suit the level and ability of the pupil. At a more advanced level for instance, pupils could be asked to name four items which can be found in the bathroom or to name four activities which can take place in the bathroom.

Board games

Simple board games provide an opportunity for pupils to repeat single words or phrases. Pupils can make their own boardgames, which will give them extra incentive and an opportunity to personalise their learning.

Example:

Animal board game. An animal is drawn in each square, as shown on the diagram on the next page. Pupils throw a dice to see which square to land on. They simply name the animal they find on the square. There can be up to 36 or 50 squares.

- **MATCHING ACTIVITIES**

With a partner, pupils can carry out a host of matching activities which will involve repeating language over and over again. Here are a few suggestions:

Matching target language words/phrases to pictures or symbols.

Matching target language phrases to English phrases.

Matching questions to answers.

Matching quantities to items, e.g. bottle — beer, kilo — potatoes.

Matching up two halves of a sentence, e.g. when it's hot — I go to the beach.

Matching target language words to specific categories, e.g. items of furniture to various rooms in the house, items of shopping to the correct shops, foods into sweet and savoury categories, drinks into hot and cold categories, clothes into winter and summer categories.

cilt

- ### ACTING OUT OR MIMING LANGUAGE THAT TELLS A STORY

At this repetition stage, pupils are able to bring together many phrases in order to construct a sequence of events or even a complete story. By putting their own mimes/actions to these phrases (and also perhaps by setting them to music or a rap rhythm) pupils can bring this language to life and personalise what they are doing. One partner reads out the text and the other mimes the activities expressed. This activity can also work extremely well as a group exercise.

Such activities can simply comprise three or four phrases describing, for example, aspects of daily routine: *getting up in the morning; getting dressed; what happens at breakfast; journey to school or work; activities in the evening.*

However, it can also involve telling a complete story, or it can involve acting out a poem or a piece of prose.

The following poem by Jacques Prévert is excellent for miming purposes:

Déjeuner du matin	
Il a mis le café	Dans le cendrier
Dans la tasse	Sans me parler
Il a mis le lait	Sans me regarder
Dans la tasse de café	Il s'est levé
Il a mis le sucre	Il a mis
Dans le café au lait	Son chapeau sur sa tête
Avec la petite cuiller	Il a mis
Il a tourné	Son manteau de pluie
Il a bu le café au lait	Parce qu'il pleuvait
Et il a reposé la tasse	Et il est parti
Sans me parler	Sous la pluie
Il a allumé	Sans une parole
Une cigarette	Sans me regarder
Il a fait des ronds	Et moi j'ai pris
Avec la fumée	Ma tête dans ma main
Il a mis les cendres	Et j'ai pleuré.

Jacques Prévert
Extrait du livre *Paroles*, © Editions GALLIMARD

SUMMARY

This repetition stage of learning provides an excellent opportunity for pupils to practise and consolidate language learnt over a period of minutes, hours and days. It is very important for pupils to make this language their own and they can only do this by using it many times over. It is up to us as teachers to provide stimulating and varied activities for our pupils to enable and encourage them to use this language over and over again. This is why variety of activity is so important.

THE MANIPULATION STAGE

At this stage of learning pupils have an even greater opportunity to use their imagination and ingenuity. They have enough language to move away from simple repetition. They can now adapt and replace words and phrases, they can add in new language items. Thus the language they produce starts to become more individual and consequently their sense of ownership of this language increases. **It is this individuality that we must begin to foster and encourage**.

• **FREE CIRCULATION**

In this type of activity pupils can exchange opinions and information. They can also negotiate.

Example of a negotiation activity:

Each pupil tries to fill his or her diary with seven different activities for each day of the week. Each activity must be with a different person. The seven activities given to all pupils are: bowling, cinema, swimming, disco, ice-skating, going into town, going to a concert. These activities can quickly and easily be noted down by pupils in the following grid form:

Día (day)	Actividad (activity)	Hora (time)	Nombre (name)
lunes			
martes			
miércoles			
jueves			
viernes			
sábado			
domingo			

Pupils now circulate round the room trying to fill up their diary. The language used for this type of activity can obviously vary depending on the ability of the group.

Phrases to use for this activity:

¿Qué haces lunes/martes? — What are you doing on . . . (day)? (e.g. Monday, Tuesday)

Cuándo estás libre? — When are you free?

Te gustaría . . . lunes/martes? — Would you like to . . . (activity)? on Monday/Tuesday?

Te veré allí a las . . . + time. — I'll see you there at (time) am/pm.

Nos veremos a las + time . . . *en el/en la* — (name of place) Let's meet at (time/place).

The importance of this type of activity is that it allows pupils to use a range of vocabulary and phrases yet still supports and guides them within a secure framework.

- **CUE CARDS**

Cue cards provide an excellent opportunity for pupils to manipulate language. They can of course be graded in difficulty, either providing a great deal of support or merely providing a very general guide to the interaction which is to take place between pupils. Cue cards can be picture or word based, either in the target language or in English.

Picture/symbol based cue cards:

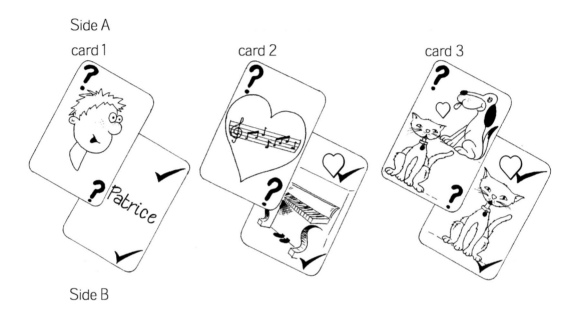

The dialogue for this cue card would be:

Side A (1)	*Comment tu t'appelles?*	(What is your name?)
Side B (1)	*Je m'appelle Patrice.*	(My name is Patrice.)
Side A (2)	*Tu aimes la musique?*	(Do you like music?)
Side B (2)	*Oui, j'aime bien la musique.*	(Yes, I really like music.
	Je joue du piano.	I play the piano)
Side A (3)	*Tu aimes les animaux?*	(Do you like animals?)
Side B (3)	*Oui. J'adore les chats.*	(Yes, I adore cats.)

CiLT

Word based cue card in the target language

NOME	1. SANDRA	2. FRANCO	3. ROSA	4. CARLO
COGNOME	CANDIOTTI	ROSSI	PONTI	MARINELLI
INDIRIZZO	ROMA ITALIA	PALERMO SICILIA	CAGLIARI SARDEGNA	NAPOLI ITALIA
FRATELLI (SORELLE)				
ANIMALE				

Using the above grid, Partner A and B take it in turns to be one of the people mentioned above. For *numero uno* (Number 1) the conversation would be as follows:

Partner A:	*Come ti chiami?*	(What is your name?)
Partner B:	*Mi chiamo Sandra Candiotti*	(My name is Sandra Candiotti.)
Partner A:	*Di dove sei?*	(Where are you from?)
Partner B:	*Sono di Roma in Italia.*	(I am from Rome in Italy.)
Partner A:	*Hai fratelli o sorelle?*	(Do you have any brothers or sisters?)
Partner B:	*Si, ho una sorella e un fratello.*	(Yes, I have one sister and one brother.)
Partner A:	*Hai un animale?*	(Have you any pets?)
Partner B:	*Si, ho un gatto.*	(Yes, I have a cat.)

The conversation based on a grid could also easily be transformed into an information gap activity with each partner having only incomplete information about each of the four people in the grid.

- ## WORD-BASED CUE CARD WITH INFORMATION IN ENGLISH

It is usually best to use symbols or the target language to stimulate responses in the target language. However, where a genuine interpreting scenario is envisaged, providing information in the mother tongue is realistic and therefore acceptable.

Example:

Pupils are told that they are working in the office of a large engineering factory that deals with Spain. They get several phone calls from Spain in the course of the day for the people listed below and have to tell the callers from Spain why they cannot speak to these people:

Mrs. Brown: Out of the office all morning visiting another factory.
              Back after lunch.

Mr Jennings: Out at lunch.
              Back at 2.30pm.

Ms Stevens: At a meeting.
              Will be available at 11.30am

Mr. Jarvis : Off sick.
              Will be back at work next week.

Sometimes the cue cards can be in the form of **general information only** and thus give the pupils much more freedom to choose what they are going to say.

Example:

Menu-based dialogues
Pupils are given a menu and given the following general guidance: *Bestell einen Imbiss und etwas zu trinken für zwei Personen* (Order a snack and something to drink for two people). Based on this information the pupils make up a dialogue between a waiter and a customer.

CiLT

Other suggestions:

Map of a town — conversation between tourist information officer and a visitor looking for places to shop/location of hotels and guest houses.

Plan of a department store — conversation between person working at customer services and shopper asking for information about where to buy certain items in the store.

Plan of a train station, airport — conversation between person at information desk and traveller trying to find a particular place.

- **ROLEPLAYS**

At this stage in the language learning process, roleplays provide an opportunity for pupils to repeat and manipulate language.

However, if we are not careful, roleplay work can degenerate into dull, meaningless repetition. Repeating large chunks of language can be very dull — there is no need to listen to what your partner is saying, all you have to do is to wait for your cue.

If this is the case, surely we should be avoiding pre-scripted roleplay work altogether?

No, roleplay is an important part of language learning. We don't always want to build in information gap work, or base our dialogues on cuecards. This could also become boring if done continually. At times pupils need to hear, read and rehearse complete dialogues.

How can we make this a stimulating and memorable experience? How can we ensure enthusiastic participation on the part of our pupils?

Here are some suggestions:

Make changes to the dialogues
All words underlined in the dialogue can be replaced by words selected by the pupils from a list of words. A pool of suitable words can be made available at the bottom of the page, on a separate sheet, on the board, on the OHP, e.g. days of the week, times, names of people, places, numbers, items of food, clothing etc.

Add emotions
Pupils act out the dialogue in an **angry**, **sad**, **frustrated**, **relaxed way** etc. Other members of the class have to guess the emotion being acted out.

CiLT

Example:

A: *Entschuldigung, dass ich so spät komme. Du wartest schon lange?*
   (I'm sorry I'm late. Have you been waiting long?)
B: *Eine halbe Stunde. Was ist denn passiert?*
   (Half an hour. What happened?)
A: *Ich war nicht daran schuld. Der Zug hatte Verspätung.*
   (It wasn't my fault. The train was late.)
B: *Na ja. Gut, dass du endlich hier bist.*
   (Oh well. It's good that you're here at last.)

Using this dialogue, pupils now assume a variety of emotions whilst playing out the dialogue, e.g.:

A= *sehr entspannt*	(very relaxed)	
B= *wütend*	(furious)	
A= *besorgt*	(anxious)	
B= *sehr höflich*	(very polite)	
A= *schlechter Laune*	(bad tempered)	
B= *ungeduldig*	(impatient)	

Use a variety of voices and/or intonations
Pupils speak like a robot, fast/slow, loud/soft, with a very high pitched voice/low voice or by mimicking someone famous like a television celebrity or cartoon character.

They could be asked to play out the dialogue as if they were very old or very young.

They could also try and mimic the voices of the two native speakers who have recorded the dialogue on cassette.

Act it out according to specified roles
Pupils assume the roles of mother and naughty child, loving couple, squabbling siblings, son or daughter with ageing parent, two business people trying to impress one another etc. The other members of the class have to guess the relationship.

Act it out in a special setting
A restaurant scene for example could be in a railway carriage (everything sliding from

side to side), on board a ship or on an aeroplane (same problem and others too?!!), in a deluxe hotel, in a training restaurant run by the local catering college, in a very cheap and cheerful café. The rest of the class have to try and guess where the role play is taking place.

Change the roleplays
Ask pupils to make changes by adding in problems, introducing additional characters, adding an unusual ending. (See Chapter 4 page 56 under heading 'Differentiation' for further ideas on adapting material.)

• **RANKING ACTIVITIES**

This type of activity involves pupils in working with ten to twenty words over and over again in a bid to decide with a partner which are the most important.

Example:

Ask pupils to select the ten most suitable items from the following list to take on a survival expedition. They have crash-landed in the middle of the Amazon jungle, and the nearest help is at least 300 miles away. From the list below the pupils select the ten most important items to take with them. They have to put these ten items in order of importance.

Un compass	(compass)
Les bandages	(bandages)
Une bouteille d'eau	(bottle of water)
Du chocolat	(chocolate)
Un fusil	(gun)
Une tente	(tent)
Une casserole	(saucepan)
Des allumettes	(matches)
Un couteau	(knife)
Une guitare	(guitar)
Une carte	(map)
Un parapluie	(umbrella)
Une corde	(rope)
Une radio	(radio)
Un sac de couchage	(sleeping bag)

A similar activity can involve pupils working out how much they can afford to buy.

Example:

Du hast nur DM 6000, um Möbel für deine erste Wohnung zu kaufen. Was kaufst du? Mach eine Liste. (You have only 6000 DM to buy furniture for your first flat. What do you buy? Make a list.) Pupils must now select which of the following items they will buy with 6000 DM (£2000):

> *der Mikrowellenofen zu DM 600* (Microwave oven at £200);
> *das Bett zu DM 900* (Bed at £250);
> *der Ofen zu DM 1050* (Oven at £300);
> *der Esstisch zu DM 450* (Dining Table at £150);
> *die Schlafcouch zu DM 1350* (Sofa Bed at £450);
> *die Waschmaschine zu DM 1050* (Washing Machine at £350);
> *der Satellitenhörer zu DM 300* (Satellite Receiver at £99);
> *der Computer zu DM 6000* (Computer at £2000);
> *das Sofa zu DM 600* (Sofa at £200);
> *der Stuhl [für das Esszimmer] zu DM 80 pro Stuhl* (Dining chairs at £30 each) etc

This type of ranking activity also allows pupils to use phrases of agreement and disagreement at this stage of learning and can indeed include some phrases of negotiation and persuasion.

SUMMARY

The manipulation stage gives pupils the confidence to use a range of language, which remains fairly tightly controlled by the teacher in structured and well defined situations.

THE PRODUCTIVE AND CREATIVE STAGE

This is the stage we want all our learners to reach — the stage at which they are able to go beyond the tight parameters we have set them before. By this stage hopefully we can allow them much more freedom to branch out and express themselves in a more creative and imaginative way.

Here are some suggestions:

- ## GRADUAL REVEALING OF A PICTURE

Partner A reveals a picture a tiny bit at a time. Partner B has been given no indication beforehand about the contents of the picture — it could be a person, an object, a scene. Partner B's aim is to work out what the picture is about with as little of the picture being revealed as possible.

This type of activity can throw up a lot of creative questions for Partner B to ask. Partner A however is restricted to **yes** and **no** answers only.

Working out what the picture is
This is a variation of the above. This time, however, the whole picture is shown to Partner B, but the picture has been partially erased. Partner B has to try and work out what the picture is about. Once again Partner A is restricted to giving just **yes** and **no** answers.

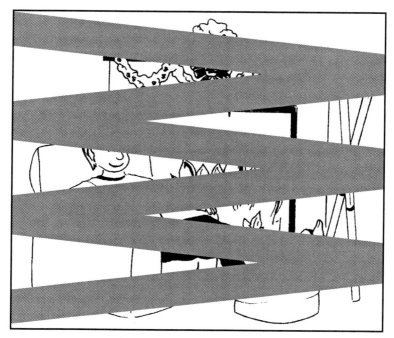

for solution see page 61

- ## FEELING AN OBJECT

An object can be placed by Partner A in a closed bag and by feeling the shape of the object Partner B has to try and guess what the item is.

- **FREE CIRCULATION ACTIVITIES**

Who am I?
Place the name of a famous person on the back of each pupil. Pupils must then circulate in the room, asking each person they meet just one question which can only be answered by yes or no. They try and find out as quickly as possible who they are.

Possible questions would be:
Bin ich eine Frau? (Am I a woman?) *Bin ich noch am Leben?* (Am I still alive?) *Bin ich Politiker?* (Am I a politician?) *Bin ich Sänger?* (Am I a singer?) *Bin ich Fernsehstar?* (Am I a TV personality?) *Habe ich einen Oscar gewonnen?* (Have I won an Oscar?)

- **DIALOGUE SIMULATIONS**

Ask pupils to create their own dialogues by providing them with different stimuli, e.g;

— a general picture stimulus only;

— a number of items, e.g. a bus ticket, two tickets to the cinema; menu from a restaurant; a wallet; a pair of washing-up gloves.

— a sketched scene, e.g., order a meal for you and your family . . . Remember however that your mum is a vegetarian and your sister hates fish!

— problem solving, e.g. invent a roleplay at a hotel reception between a very patient receptionist and a very fussy hotel guest. There are problems with the room that the guest has been given.

— questions and answers. Only the answers to a dialogue are given; pupils have to try and work out what the missing questions could be.

- **COMPARING OPINIONS/STIMULATIONG DISCUSSION**

One way to stimulate discussion is by the use of prepared written statements or opinions on a particular topic or issue, e.g. drugs, smoking, and the environment. Working in pairs, pupils place these statement cards under 'agree', 'disagree' or 'not sure' headings. Following on from this, discussion can be encouraged about where the statements were placed or the issues themselves.

CiLT

- **JUST A MINUTE!**

How many complaints can you make in a minute? This activity can be based in a variety of settings — a hotel, a restaurant, a campsite, a clothes shop, a leisure centre etc.

- **TWENTY QUESTIONS**

If necessary, help can be provided in the form of information cards giving the person's name, when they lived, their nationality, their job. A number of these cards (approx. ten or more depending on the level and ability of the group) are then placed face up. Partner A decides upon a card (unknown to Partner B). Partner B starts to ask questions to find out in less than twenty questions (all of which must be answered by yes or no) which person Partner A is pretending to be.

- **RANKING ACTIVITY**

At this stage of language learning, ranking activities can now involve pupils justifying the order in which they place a list of items/ideas etc. To help pupils give the reasons for their choice, a list of written statements should be provided.

- **IDENTIFICATION ACTIVITIES**

Identifying items in a picture
In this activity Partner A and Partner B together make a list of the various items they can see in a picture of a room. This can be either an oral or a written activity. Once they have made the list they have to decide what type of person might live in that room and identify that person from a selection of photographs of people which they have been given. Clues could be given for the rooms as follows:

supermodel — *fashion magazines, glitzy clothes*
pop singer — *karaoke machine, music scores*
explorer — *compass, maps*
artist — *paintbrushes, canvases, paint*
teacher — *pile of exercise books!*

Which picture am I describing?
Partner A describes only one of a series of very similar looking pictures (of different people, of groups of people, of outdoor scenes, of rooms in a house). Partner B must identify as quickly as possible which picture is being described.

Find the differences
Partner A and Partner B both have pictures which are very similar, but there are several differences. Neither is allowed to look at the other's picture. By talking to each other about their pictures, they have to try and work out what the differences are. They make a list of the differences. Once they have completed the list of differences, they look at each other's picture to see if their list is correct.

• DRAW WHAT YOU HEAR

Partner A has a picture which Partner B cannot see. The picture may be of a person, a group of people involved in an activity, or a scene, etc. Partner A describes the picture to Partner B who must draw what s/he hears.

• BUILD/SET UP ACCORDING TO THE INSTRUCTIONS YOU HEAR

Partner A has a diagram of the layout of furniture in a room. Partner B has the items of furniture (dolls' furniture) which s/he must place according to the instructions given by Partner A.

• DESCRIBE A PHOTO

Pupils bring in photos of themselves and their friends and/or families. In pairs they tell each other about the people in their photos.

• GAMES

At this stage of language production we want to encourage pupils to speak freely on a variety of topics, therefore games based on the following ideas are ideal:

Boardgame
Speak for a minute: On each square of a boardgame is a topic area, e.g. *moi, mon école, où j'habite* (me, my school, where I live). If you land on a particular square you have to speak for a minute on that particular topic.

CiLT

Card game

This game consists of a set of cards with a different situation on each card. These situations all require pupils to respond with some sort of reaction. As outlined below, partners take it in turns to react to the situations on the cards their partner turns up.

Partner A takes the top card from the set which is placed face-down on the table. S/he must read out the situation and the partner must then choose an appropriate reaction, e.g. *Ich habe meine Uhr verloren* (I've lost my watch). The partner must now make up an appropriate reaction to the situation.

List of possible situations:

Ich habe meine Stelle verloren.	(I have lost my job.)
Ich habe £250,000 gewonnen.	(I have won £250,000.)
Mein Wellensittich ist gestorben.	(My budgie has died.)
Morgen fahre ich nach Amerika.	(I'm going to America tomorrow.)
Ich habe schreckliches Zahnweh.	(I have terrible toothache.)
Wie findest du the Spice Girls?	(What do you think of the Spice Girls?)
Morgen mache ich Prüfungen.	(My exams are tomorrow.)

Possible reactions which pupils might be expected to make to these situations:

Die sind toll!	(They're great)
Die sind schrecklich!	(They're terrible)
Das tut mir leid!	(I'm sorry)
Pech!	(Bad luck)
Viel Glück!	(Best of luck)
Ich gratuliere!	(Congratulations)

At a less advanced stage of learning this could also form the basis of a matching activity where the situation cards are matched up with a set of previously prepared 'reaction' cards.

- VOCABULARY-ENHANCING ACTIVITIES

The following activities are all designed to stimulate the need and desire for the acquisition of new and exciting vocabulary! Pupils can be encouraged to use their dictionaries for these activities:

Word association
Word association games can be an excellent way to enlarge vocabulary.

Word chains
Partner A selects any word in the target language, e.g. *grande*. Partner B must now select a word which begins with the last letter of that word. In this case the letter 'e', e.g. *enero*. Partner A must now think of a word which begins with 'o' e.g. *organisación* . . . and so it continues.

Describing the cat
Pupils take it in turn to find adjectives to describe their imaginary cat. The adjectives are chosen alphabetically, e.g. Partner A starts by using the letter A . . .

Partner A:	*Mon chat est aveugle.*	(My cat is blind.)
Partner B:	*Mon chat est beau.*	(My cat is beautiful.)
Partner A:	*Mon chat est curieux etc.*	(My cat is curious.)

Alphabet links
In this game pupils take it in turn to give information about a person, a country and something they buy — all of which must begin with the same letter. The letter can be selected at random by landing on a square on a boardgame, the turn of an alphabet wheel, etc, e.g.:

<u>M</u>ichael ist nach <u>M</u>alta gefahren, um <u>M</u>asken zu kaufen.
(Michael went to Malta to buy masks.)

- STORY-BASED ACTIVITIES

At this stage of learning pupils will be able to use all sorts of different language, and what better way to encourage this than by getting them to create their own stories and dialogues?

Here are a few ideas:

Alphabet conversations

Partner A and B have a conversation starting with any letter of the alphabet selected at random (out of a hat, a letter wheel, by the teacher etc). They then proceed to have as natural a conversation as possible with their partner, taking it in turn to select the first word of each sentence which begins with the appropriate letter of the alphabet, until they have used all 26 letters in the alphabet to start their sentences.

Example:

The letter chosen at random to start the conversation is the letter **L**. Thus the conversation might go something like this:

Partner A: *Letztes Jahr bin ich nach Deutschland gefahren.*
             (Last year I went to Germany.)
Partner B: *Mallorca habe ich besucht.*
             (I visited Majorca)
Partner A: *Nicht schlecht. Wie war es in Mallorca?*
             (Not bad. What was it like in Majorca?)
Partner B: *Okay. Wie war es in Deutschland?*
             (OK – what was it like in Germany?)
Partner A: *Pizzarestaurants gab es sehr viele.*
             (There were lots of pizza restaurants.)

The conversation continues up to the letter **Z** and carries on with **A**, **B**, etc. until they reach the letter **K** and therefore all 26 letters have been used.

Chain stories

In pairs, pupils take it in turns to make up sentences for a story. The story they tell is based on objects (realia), picture flashcards, words or phrases on cards.

These objects or cards can either be taken pot-luck fashion out of a hat or bag, so that the pupils don't know in advance what word/phrase they are going to have to include in each sentence; or they may all be set out in front of the pupils at the beginning of the exercise and the pupils then select what they wish as the story unfolds.

Guess what I didn't do stories

In this activity pupils give one another information about themselves, e.g. about their family, their home, what they did at the weekend, about what they did on holiday. *All the information they give must be true except for one thing.* Their partner has to try and guess what the false piece of information is.

Summary

In this final stage of learning — the creative and productive stage — opportunities have been created for pupils to use language both freely and imaginatively in situations which, where appropriate, are either very loosely structured or totally without structure.

CiLT

3. Pairwork based on mixed skills other than mainly speaking

When we think of pupils working in pairs, we tend too often to restrict the activities to the practice and consolidation of the spoken language in the main. This is a pity, as working with a partner, using the whole range of all four skills, can contribute to very meaningful, stimulating and worthwhile language work.

Although the major part of this book has been devoted primarily to activities where speaking plays the major role, here are a few ideas for pairwork activities where *speaking* will be part of the activity, but where another skill or combination of skills is also very much to the fore.

 READING AND/OR LISTENING

Activities for reading and listening have been categorised together as the type of tasks for both are in many cases the same.

THE IMITATION AND REPETITION STAGE

- **READ/LISTEN AND DRAW**

Ask the pupils to illustrate a piece of text with a series of pictures to show what is happening. Alternatively, the illustrations can be an integral part of the text which makes the text visually much more exciting.

In this example the original text was:

> *Ich wohne in einem schönen Haus* (I live in a nice house). *Das Haus ist von einem Wald umgeben* (The house is surrounded by a forest). *Unser Garten ist auch sehr schön* (Our garden is also very nice). *Im Garten sind ein großer Apfelbaum und viele schöne Blumen* (In the garden there is a large apple tree and there are many lovely flowers).

Pupils, working in pairs, must now rewrite the text, but use a picture for every word underlined. The result would be something like this:

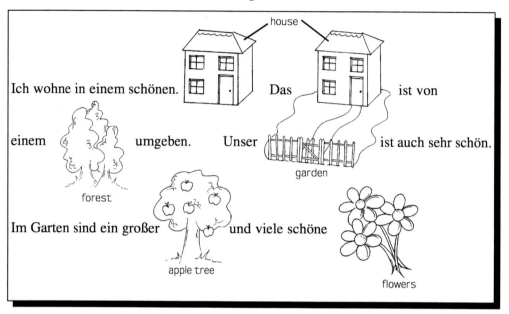

- **UNJUMBLE**

Pupils are given a picture of rooms in a house, but the labels for the various rooms are in the wrong place. Together the pupils must rearrange the labels so that it all makes sense. This can also be done with parts of the body, countries in Europe, shops, pieces of furniture in the wrong rooms, etc.

- **CATEGORISE**

Get pupils to put words or phrases given to them on the OHP or on a sheet of paper into certain categories.

This could be very simply listing pieces of furniture according to the rooms in which you find them, listing foods into the categories of sweet and savoury, arranging items according to the shop where you would find them, categorising activities into indoor and outdoor.

- **NUMBER DICTATION**

Partner A calls out a series of numbers in the target language. Partner B must note these numbers down.

Telephone numbers

Strictly speaking this is a chain activity. It provides excellent listening practice as well as a very good opportunity to say numbers aloud.

Each pupil is given a card with two telephone numbers on it.

```
01 69 09 90 64
04 76 95 97 37
```

The top number represents their own telephone number. The number at the bottom of the card is the number they wish to call. The activity starts by a pupil calling out to the rest of the class the top number on their card:

Mon numéro de téléphone est 01 69 09 90 64. They then tell the rest of the class the number they are trying to contact:

Je voudrais contacter le numéro suivant: 04 76 95 97 37.
(I wish to contact telephone number 04 76 95 97 37.)

Everyone else in the class has to listen very intently to hear whether their telephone number is the number which is being called out. If it is, the pupil responds by shouting out: 04 76 95 97 37 — *ça, c'est mon numéro de téléphone* (that is my telephone number) and s/he then proceeds to tell the rest of the class the telephone number s/he is looking for. The activity continues until all pupils have heard and identified their own telephone number and called out the number they are looking for.

N.B. before doing 'Telephone numbers' as a class activity, pupils will need to be taught how telephone numbers are read aloud in various languages. For French say that numbers are read aloud in pairs, e.g. 01 69 09 90 64 would be read out as follows: zéro un, soixante-neuf, zéro neuf, quatre-vingt-dix, soixante-quatre.

THE MANIPULATION STAGE

• GIVE ME INFORMATION!

An example of this is the tourist information guide game. Partner A plays the tourist wanting information on a certain topic, e.g. sights, hotels, restaurants, leisure activities.

Partner B — the tourist information officer — has all the information in his or her guide book. S/he now has to scan the information to give his/her partner the information s/he requires.

- **MATCHING QUESTIONS TO ANSWERS PLUS RE-ORDERING ACTIVITY**

This is a type of dialogue/questionnaire activity where the questions and answers are jumbled up. Working together, Partners A and B work out which question goes with which answer. Once this is done, they have to put the questions and answers into a sensible order. The final stage of this activity is to roleplay the dialogue.

THE PRODUCTION/CREATIVITY STAGE

- **READ AND COMPARE**

In this activity two pupils are given a text to read together. Their first task is to list the words and phrases from the text which they do not understand. They then work together with a dictionary to check meanings. Alternatively, the teacher brainstorms the various pairs and all new vocabulary is explained and written on the board. Pupils are then given a list of written statements about the text. They are asked to decide whether they agree or disagree with each statement and, where appropriate, to give a reason for their answer.

- **READ AND ROLEPLAY**

Partner A and B read a text together. They then roleplay the situation they have just read about, e.g. they have read a letter and now one partner plays the person who has written the letter and the other partner asks the letter writer questions.

 WRITING

THE IMITATION/REPETITION STAGE

- **DRAW AND LABEL**

Pupils can work together on a whole variety of labelling activities, e.g. drawing and labelling parts of the body, items of clothing, buildings in the town, plan of a school, shops in a shopping centre, items found in various shops. This can be extended to phrases and sentences to describe a sequence of activities.

- **MEMORISE AND COPY**

Partner A and Partner B memorise a list of words for a couple of minutes, e.g. a shopping list, items of clothes to pack for an adventure holiday, a list of items to bring when going camping, contents of a medical box, pieces of furniture for a new flat. Each partner then puts the list out of sight and independently writes it down from memory. They then compare lists with each other before checking with the original to see if they have remembered all the items.

- **CATEGORISE**

Pupils work together in pairs to compose lists of words or phrases under various headings. This can be a type of brainstorming activity and the results can be fed back to the teacher or to another pair of pupils, e.g. 'Write down the names of five items you could buy in a fruit shop.', 'Six phrases you would need when booking into an hotel.' etc.

THE MANIPULATION STAGE

- **SELECT AND COPY**

From a pool of phrases and words the pupils, working in pairs, select words and phrases to compile a dialogue or a description.

- **ADAPT A DIALOGUE/POSTER/DESCRIPTION**

This involves changing the text by changing words and phrases – altering times, dates, people's names, etc.

- **MAKE A DIALOGUE FROM A GRID**

In this activity information is provided in grid form. Pupils are required to construct a dialogue based on this information, as in the following example:

Doctor with a young patient

1	?	Doktor
2	˃Ͼ Ͽ˂	Patient
3	Tage?	Doktor
4	2	Patient
5	🤒 ? 🤒 ?	Doktor
6	Nein	Patient
	(Der Doktor untersucht den Patient) (doctor examines patient)	
7	Virus — nicht schlimm	Doktor
	◑◑ x 3 täglich	Doktor
8	Danke	Patient
9	Auf Wiedersehen	Patient/Doktor

1 *Was ist los*? (What is the matter?)

2 *Ich habe Ohrenschmerzen.* (I have earache.)

3 *Seit wann hast du das?* (How long have you had it?)

4 *Seit zwei Tagen.* (For two days.)

5 *Hast du auch andere Symptome — Kopfweh oder Halsschmerzen zum Beispiel?*
(Have you also other symptoms — e.g. headache or a sore throat?)

6 *Nein. (Der Arzt untersucht die Ohren des Patienten.)*
No. (Doctor examines patient's ears.)

7 *Du hast ein Virus. Es ist nichts Schlimmes. Ich verschreibe dir Tabletten. Nimm zwei*
Tabletten dreimal täglich nach dem Essen. (You have a virus. It's nothing serious.
I am prescribing tablets for you. Take two tablets three times daily, after meals.)

8 *Danke, Herr Doktor.* (Thank you, doctor.)

9 *Auf Wiedersehen.* (Goodbye.)

CiLT

THE PRODUCTIVE AND CREATIVE STAGE

- CREATE A DIALOGUE/POSTER/DESCRIPTION

- CREATE A BOARDGAME

A basic blank boardgame layout allows pupils to create and practise a wide variety of structures and situations through making up instructions for their own boardgame.

- CREATE A STORY

Pupils are given a series of pictures. In pairs, pupils decide what is going on in each picture and write some sentences to describe each picture. They then put the pictures into what they consider is the correct order. Once this is done they record their story.

Alternatively, they can create pictures within the text (see *Read/listen and draw* on page 49).

- WORK OUT WHAT'S MISSING

Pupils can be given a dialogue which has been partially erased, e.g. parts of words missing, some words missing altogether. Working in pairs, pupils have to try and work out the missing pieces and write out the complete dialogue.

- START A DIALOGUE/FINISH A DIALOGUE/MAKE UP THE MISSING PARTS OF THE DIALOGUE

In this case, pupils have to work out from the text they have in front of them what might be in the missing sections. They then create the missing sections.

SUMMARY

The activities described in this section represent merely the tip of a most substantial iceberg. The list could indeed be limitless, as any activity which we ask our pupils to do can be undertaken as a paired activity.

4. A final checklist for the teacher

In this chapter we look at three key aspects which in many cases must feature if pairwork is to be successful.

 ## 1. DIFFERENTIATION

The importance of providing differentiated tasks for pairwork activities cannot be overstated. Providing tasks graded in difficulty is important when compiling activities for listening, reading and writing. It is equally important for speaking activities.

Pairwork provides an ideal opportunity to introduce differentiated tasks.

Successful pairwork must always aim to provide meaningful and stimulating activities.

For different pupils this will entail different things. The pairwork activity must provide the following:

1) A task which is meaningful to the pupils, a task in which there is a clear purpose.

2) A starter task which is accessible to all pupils.

3) Possibilities of going beyond the basic task.

This may entail providing tasks graded in difficulty as well as providing a variety of tasks (*differentiation by task*). The activity may on the other hand be an open-ended task which pupils tackle at their own level (*differentiation by outcome*).

Example:

In the restaurant conversation on page 16 we looked at various ways to introduce graded tasks. Here is a summary of these tasks:

- words for the various foods and drinks can be substituted;
- prices can be changed;

- additional items can be ordered;
- extra people can be added in;
- problems can be added e.g. one of your party is a vegetarian, you receive the wrong change, your soup is cold — you ask for it to be heated up. The beef is tough — you ask the waiter to give you something else;
- pupils can be asked to create their own dialogues based on the dialogues they have just read;
- pupils can be asked to create cue cards for the dialogues they have created themselves. These cuecards can then be used by other pupils to work out the original dialogues;

Building in differentiated tasks means that all pupils are challenged, stimulated and stretched. This is vital for successful pairwork.

 ## 2. AUTONOMOUS LEARNING

Mention has already been made of the importance of preparing pupils in the whole class situation for what they will eventually do in pairs. It was stressed that they should be independent of the teacher once they start to work in pairs. However, total independence will not always be achievable through thorough whole class preparation alone. Other steps need to be taken when pupils are working with their partners to ensure that they are getting the most out of the work that they are doing and that they have the means to get help for themselves.

Here are some ideas to aid autonomous learning:

- provide help sheets for those who need them;
- provide answer sheets so that pupils can correct work themselves;
- provide checklists/model answers which pupils can refer to when necessary;
- encourage pupils to use the dictionary;
- provide a series of tasks graded in difficulty so that pupils can work at their own pace;
- where appropriate, provide pupils with a choice of activity;
- foster an atmosphere of independent learning in your classroom. This can only be done over a period of time.

If you do not train your pupils to work autonomously, your opportunities for pairwork are very limited.

3. MONITORING PAIRWORK

Up to now emphasis has been on the materials, the activities and the pupils. What about the teacher? What is their role when pairwork is taking place?

- **MONITORING TO HELP AND PRAISE**

Pupils must feel that the pairwork tasks are worth doing. Thus the teacher's comments and monitoring are vital. This is the time to:

- help weak pupils;
- stretch more able pupils;
- encourage less confident pupils;
- praise pupils;
- get to know pupils.

- **MONITORING TO ASSESS**

At times the teacher will also need to assess the speaking skills of the pupils and this can be incorporated into the normal pairwork activities. It can be done in two ways:

- The teacher eavesdrops on the pairwork activity of the pupils s/he wishes to assess.
- Pairs of pupils can be formally assessed by the teacher at the front of the class.

Whichever method is used, it means that assessment can be easily integrated into the normal pattern of working.

SUMMARY

Differentiated learning, autonomous learning and the teacher's role of monitoring are all central to successful pairwork. Without them pairwork may well prove to be a very negative experience for many pupils. If they are built in, however, working with a partner will result in a very stimulating and worthwhile activity.

Conclusion

In summary . . .

- Pairwork, provides the medium for one of the most natural forms of communication and ways of working in the real world — the one-to-one — and should be an integral part of the learning process in the classroom.

- Pairwork is applicable at all stages of language learning and therefore can be easily integrated into any stage of the learning process.

- Pairwork can be a mixed skills activity focusing in particular on any one or more of the four attainment targets.

- Successful pairwork is totally dependent on thorough whole class preparation.

- Pairwork can be a simple 30-second imitation of what the teacher has just said and what the whole class has just repeated. However, this type of activity represents merely the first, although wholly satisfying and stable rung of a very long and interesting ladder.

At the top of the ladder pupils are working together for extended periods of time on a range of activities, such as:

- creating their own highly individual language;

- reacting in an objective, subjective, personal or analytical fashion to language they have just heard or read;

- reacting to language that a neighbouring pair of fellow pupils has just written.

The possibilities on the top rungs of the ladder are limitless and very exciting.

- No really satisfying and meaningful pairwork can be achieved unless pupils are taught how to work in pairs. They have to learn to be flexible in terms not only of what they do and how they do it, but also accept that they must be prepared to work with any one of their classmates at various times. The need to be flexible and adaptable in terms of who they work with is of key importance.

References

INTRODUCTION

1 BBC INSET Programme, *The communicative classroom*, notes for teachers (BBC, 1988)

2 Beyer G., *Gedächtnis und Konzentrationstraining* (Econ Verlag, Düsseldorf/Wien) cited by Tumber, M. in 'Developing Pupil Autonomy', *ALL Language Learning Journal No. 4* (1991)

3 Ur, P., *A course in language teaching, practice and theory* (CUP, 1996)

4 Buckby M. et al., Jones B., Berwick G, *Learning Strategies*, Teacher Manual, (Collins Educational, 1992)

5 *MFL in the national curriculum* (DFE, 1995)

CHAPTER ONE

1 Ur, P., *A course in language teaching, practice and theory* (CUP, 1996)

CHAPTER TWO

1 Buckby M. et al., *Strategies* (Collins, 1992)

CiLT

Solution to picture puzzle on page 41.